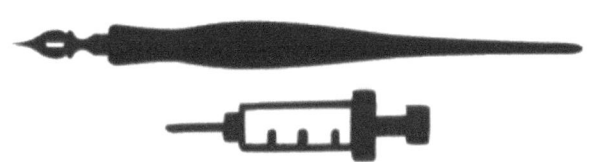

Medicine for the Marrow

A 30-Day Writing Challenge

Phoebe Eligon-Jones

Blupoetres Creations

MEDICINE FOR THE MARROW

Dedication

To everyone and no one.
To writers of the block.
To anyone who's ever been stuck.
To my poetic family at Write About Now Facebook
member's page.

Write with me...

Table of Contents

Day 1 – Prompt: Write a poem using only questions.

Why do you hate me?

Do I remind you of that part of yourself that you hate?
Or is it something more like a cold, perhaps common?
Is it that you despise the color of my skin?
Sorry, would that make you racist?
Are you afraid to admit the awful truth?
Does it frighten you to learn this about yourself?
How could you not know?

> Do you cross the street when you see a Black
> man coming towards you?
> Do you clutch your purse when a Black woman
> joins you on an elevator ride?
> Do you relish telling people you have one Black
> friend or family member?
> Do you think Black afros, braids, or locs are
> unprofessional?
> Do you feel uncomfortable when you see Black
> teenagers playing together?
> Do you believe any Black person, including
> children, killed by the police should
> "just comply"?

Did you answer "yes" to any of those questions?
Is the answer still not obvious?
You don't even know why, do you?
What about your mama, daddy, meemaw or any of your kin?
Does their hate match yours or was it passed down like
grandpa's guns?
Who's hanging from your family tree?
Do they resemble anyone like me?
Is that what's got you so distraught?
That we'll find out exactly who you really are?
Is it remotely possible that we already know?
Did you honestly think your hate was a secret?
I wonder, what else are you hiding?

Bobbie

Barbie, you ain't shit and neither is Ken
With your blond hair and blue eyes that didn't look anything like
        me or mine
I had your mansion and your car
And I still couldn't picture myself in them
Your big titties, micro-waist, and non-existent ass stayed
        plastered on every toy store shelf
Feet perpetually pointed for high heel shoes
What little girl was out in them streets in stilettos, Barbie, hm?
Back then, there was an outfit for every occasion:
        Swimming, dancing, the holidays, entertaining
Nothing about a career for years, but you had accessories, right?
        Sunglasses, rings, hats, gloves, wraps
Bitch, you had more shit than this Black girl's mama was willing
        to buy
For years, I would get a different version of you as gifts
What little girl wouldn't want you?
My friends envied me for having you
What were they really envious of:
        Your fake ass portrayal of the perfect woman?
But you weren't perfect…until 1980
The box even said:
        BLACK BARBIE
As if it wasn't fucking obvious by the curly Afro and coffee-
        colored limbs
The seven-year-old joy, excitement, and pride I felt died just as
        quickly
Why do you think that is, you selfish bitch?
Because it would take another three fucking years to get a Black
        Barbie that looked like me or mine
The stores kept her hidden, the boxes never delivered to my
        Toys R Us, Woolworth or Alexander's
For that, I will always hate you for keeping me away from
Bobbie

Yeah, I changed Black Barbie's name the second I tore her out
     of the box
So, fuck you Barbie and your no-dick having Ken

Day 3 – Prompt: Poem using "magic, mundane, marrow".

Mutual

It was the magic of the moment
No more mundane than Monday mornings
The moon majestically made the night come alive
Emotions no longer manageable or measurable
Maybe trying to master the matter was futile
The message, no the meaning of it, melted my heart
Mercy me, the memory of his marriage proposal:
       Medicine for the marrow
Upon the midnight hour, he murdered much
Making him mine, and our future a mystery

Day 4 – Prompt: Look around the room you're sitting in. Pick an object, write from its perspective.

Cast Away

I know she sees me sitting here
Walks past me at least five times a day
I'm here!
Hello!
Got me stuck in this cup with these ragamuffin wannabes
Doesn't she remember how special I am?
> Bright white pearlized casing
> Silver tips on each end
> Royal blue blood coursing through my body
How could she forget me here?
We were writing together so beautifully
> It was a Tuesday
> The sky overcast
> Her lips were upturned in the faintest smile
> The phone rang and she left me on the desk
But then…
But then…
She didn't come back
And her husband, her simple, non-writing lover, manhandled
me
He touched me in the most unpleasant manner
Rough hands lifting me and inspecting my craftsmanship
I vaguely heard him mutter:
> "Geez, not another pen"
Pen?
Pen?!
How dare he classify me with such frivolity
> I am a calligrapher's dream
> A poet's life line
> An author's muse
How dare he?!
Now I'm here, trapped
Lost in a sea of basic banality

I can feel my base squishing in the murky ink of my inferior
          comrades
This is not fair
I demand justice
Free me or suffer the repercussions.

Day 5 – Prompt: Write a haiku about your hands.

Hand Over Fist

What I write about
Ain't none of your damn business
Lest I come for you.

Day 6 – Prompt: Write a poem that ends with "I was wrong. I was wrong".

Not Okay

I am fine
No, really, I'm fine
I have my health
Well, sort of
I have a great job
But I wouldn't mind better
I have a banging body
Oops, I actually need to lose 30lbs
I have a beautiful home
Don't come over, though, it's filthy
I have not a care in the world
That's a lie, anxiety runs my life
Maybe, I'm not fine
I was wrong
I was wrong.

Day 7 – Prompt: Write a poem titled "Erase".

Erase

If I block you, don't be offended
Isn't that what you said:
"No offense"?
Right before you said something offensive
I don't have to take your shit
                                          Not your negativity
                                              Not your hate
     Not your bitchassfuckingcomplainingabouteveryfuckingthingIdo
I don't have to take you
So, rather than offend you
I shall erase you
And think of you no more.

Day 8 – Prompt: Write a dialogue poem, but only show us one side of the conversation. You could write both sides and then omit one or just write one side and imagine the rest! Be creative!

Respect on a Name

Ay, yo, Miss, can I ask you somethin'?
Ai'ight Teacher
But you are the teacher, tho
You really askin' for a lot
It ain't that serious
You can't do that!
Well, cuz you're the teacher
Y'all teachers really be askin' for the most
Why? You call me sir or Mr. X all the time
Nah, see you just pushing your agenda
Oh, I'm a scholar now?
Two seconds ago, you threatened to call me out my name
So, what?
Now you're a sociologist?
Just had to correct me
I guess not
You talk to all your students like this?
Oh, word?
Ai'ight Miss, I mean, Mrs. Teacher.
Is that better?
Damn, my bad.
I forgot the question.

Day 9 – Prompt: Write a poem from the perspective of your favorite book.

Thesis

You just finished my last page
The sigh that escaped your lips less audible than your heartbeat
I watch as you lean back, lost in thought or emotion
You take a long deep breath
Fingers dragging heavily through your locs
Your eyes, barely slits, offer up dueling tears on the same cheek
You don't brush them away, rather allow them to fall upon me
Warmth and salt like the sea travel the expanse to my final
        punctuation
Once your eyes open, I can't quite measure what I see
A deluge of wet trembles behind rapid flickers of lashes
Concerned, I can't tell the difference:
        Delight or outrage
        Revulsion or hysteria
        Pleasure or misery
Just when I think I'll go mad trying to guess
You deliver my resolve
It wasn't noticeable at first
A distant rumble of mirth rising from your diaphragm
Before I could process what was happening
You grabbed me close to your bosom
Breath and archive becoming one
You whisper:

        It is done.

Day 10 – Prompt: Pick an older poem of yours, turn this poem into an erasure poem. Bonus if you use a poem you wrote in the previous 9 days of our challenge! https://poets.org/glossary/erasure

Non-Classified

You hate me
I remind you of that part of yourself that you hate
Like a cold, common
You despise my skin
Sorry, racist
Admit the awful truth
It frightens you to learn this about yourself
Could you not…
    Cross the street when a Black man coming towards you
    Clutch purse when a Black woman joins you on an
        elevator ride
    Relish telling people you have one Black friend or family
        member
    Think Black afros, braids, or locs are unprofessional
    Feel uncomfortable when you see Black teenagers playing
        together
    Believe any Black person, including children, killed by the
        police should "just comply"
The answer still obvious
You don't even know why
Your mama, daddy, meemaw or kin
Their hate matches yours
Passed down like grandpa's guns
Hangings from your family tree
They resemble me
That's got you distraught
Exactly who you really are
We already know
Your hate was a secret
What else are you hiding?

Day 11 – Prompt: Write a poem inspired by the person or people you compare yourself to and/or are jealous of.

I Want What They Got

At this moment, I need a pause button. My minutes, hours, days seem to pass by at infinite speed. I need to slow things down. Is that grass outside? Is it even green? Are there flowers for me to stop to smell?

At this moment, I need a break from myself. Constantly moving but not really going anywhere. Someone discover me. Fund me. Put me on the cover of something. Although that wouldn't actually give me a break. Dammit.

At this moment, I need to win the lottery. Buy a private island in middle of the ocean. Sandy beaches all around. The things that money could do for me. Then, everyone else would come for me.

At this moment, I just really want what they got. Whoever the theys are. Whatever the theys have, I simply have to have it.

Day 12 – Prompt: Poem with repeated line "I forget" and "I remember".

Echo

I forget sometimes that my glasses are on my head
But I remember how our first date lasted for hours

I forget where I put my keys only to find them hanging from my purse
But I remember how your hands feel hours after you go to work

I forget how to make the simplest recipe so I consult YouTube
But I remember the sound of your laugh even when sleeping

I forget on an almost daily basis the Wi-Fi, or really any, password
But I remember I feel safest when I'm with you

Day 13 – Prompt: Haiku about your favorite candy.

Betwixt

Gimme left or right
Chocolate caramel goodness
Lick my fingers clean

Day 14 – Prompt: Make up a holiday and why we would celebrate it.

National Don't Give a Fuck Day

Today shall be a day like no other
There shall still be work, but we won't fucking go
We're not calling in sick, cuz fuck it
Bills still need to be paid, no worries, we ain't paying 'em
Spouse and kids asking for our time but fuck them, too
Dinner needs to be on the table, except it's gonna be takeout

Today when someone cuts you off in traffic, don't cuss or
        swear: cut them off and leave your car right the fuck
        there
Should your dog snatch your cookies: dump the rest of the box
        on floor, and stomp them to oblivion
Stay in bed, don't shower, turn your phone on "Do Not Fuck
        with me" and don't you move unless the house is on
        fucking fire
You earned this, you deserve this, so tell the world: Fuck off!

Stop for Directions

I'm lost driving on empty in search of the perfect verse
The gas tank flashes "CONFLICT CONFLICT" but I continue
        on the fumes of irony
The yellow and white poetic lines of the highway roll pass the
        scene outside my point-of-view
Metaphors and similes zoom past me doing 90 rhymes per
        minute
My hands grip the writing wheel while trying to steady my car –
ma told me to slow down and I wish I had listened –
5.0. just sauntered up behind me
Red lights flashing, sirens blaring
Demanding that I
                "REFRAIN"
                "REFRAIN"
But I can't
I won't allow myself to be taken by the –
Man, did you see that?!
Some hyperbole just swerved in front of me!
             OXYMORON!
I swear I saw my lyrics flash before my eyes
As the shock of the plot wore off, I realized the cops were
        gone…
It's a good thing, too
I already had points on my creative license
If I got caught writing under the influence, they would have
        revoked it for sure and impounded my pen of steel
I decided to get out of the fast lane since I just missed the exits
        for Stanza and Haiku
My mood was lifting as the setting of the sun on the horizon
        became the climax of my all too hectic ride
Off in the distance

Illuminated by purples oranges blues and yellows was the
        symbol I'd been searching for
I pulled up to the pump and anxiously filled up on
        Verse
                After
                        Verse
                                After
                                        Verse
A smile crept on my face as I walked in to pay
But quickly vanished when my ATM card read:
                "TRAGEDY"

                        But that's a whole other anecdote.

Day 16 – Prompt: Write a playful/humorous poem about a serious topic.

She Dead

Karen is dead. The pasty
president of the mayo militia
was pronounced dead at 4:20
am on National Don't Give a
Fuck Day. It is reported that
Karen was knocked the fuck
out when she tried to call
Tyrone to come get his negro
friends. His five fingers had a
long conversation with her dry
ass plastic puss. Karen thought
she could bring her fuckery to
the hood and insisted, "Don't
you know who my father is?"
Hey, illegally blond two and a
half, nobody cares. She chose
the wrong one to micro-
aggressively pass her bullshit
on. The Blackhanded beat
down that was unleashed upon
her all-lives matter muffin top
was voted on and approved.
With her unseasoned no-
tastebud having, couldn't catch
a beat unless it was rammed
halfway down her throat,
melanin deficient hipster ass.
"You shoulda just complied,
Karen, by leaving all Black
folks' names out of your
privileged lip-injected mouth".

Says Who?

Truth be told anybody can be an artist
Just put some paint on a brush and draw your little heart out
Little kids do it all the time
It can't be that hard, right?
That's what they say about parenting, teaching, and writing
That it's soooooo easy, right?
Just have unprotected sex with someone, boom:
$$\text{You're a mama}$$
Throw some lessons together and stand in front a class, wham:
$$\text{You're a teacher}$$
Take random words, write them down on paper, TADA:
$$\text{You're a writer}$$
Truth be told, nothing is as easy as you may think
Stop telling people that their gifts are that black and white
I dare *you* to create something beautfiul.

Day 18 – Prompt: A poem with ending line "almost there".

Impatient

I need it to be over
The constant nagging
The begging and crying
I don't remember being

> This needy
> This whiny
> This irresponsible at your age

You're an adult for crying out loud
Isn't this what you wanted?
Isn't this what you said would change everything?
Adulthood was going to change your life
And everyone's around you
But it hasn't
Has it?
How many times do I still hear myself saying:

> Grow up

The time has come
I can't keep doing this for you
Being there all the time
I know I'm supposed to
All the time
But I'm exhausted
Adulthood is calling you
You're almost there

Day 19 – Prompt: A poem from the perspective of
Friday/weekend.

TGI – Me

I've been dealing with this my whole life
Can't Thursday take over for a change
He's just as nice
The precursor to the weekend
He's my eve
You can take off on him, too, you know
Give yourself a four-day weekend
Instead of three
Don't get me wrong
I used to love all the attention
But it's all the time
There are seven of us
It can't always be just me
I get it
Everybody hates Monday
Shit, so do I
We can totally leave that bitch out
But the twins, Tuesday and Wednesday, are good people
Admit it
You love hump day
She's the sexiest day of any week
And I can say that cause she's my sister
Let's celebrate her more
Use her for some much needed
Brown-chicken-brown-cow
My parents don't need to know
Saturday and Sunday are old school
You know, Saturday, my dad, is all about the good time
While mom, the holy roller Sunday, loves church, dinner and rest
Anyway, I've tried in vain for years
I'm Friday, and if it's alright with you
I'm taking a self-care vacation

Day 20 – Prompt: Haiku to your child.

Growth

Download recipe
You've had more than enough time
Cook your own damn food

Day 21 – Prompt: Haiku about writing.

Composition

Paper, my sweet love
Today, mentally prepare
Tomorrow, we write

Day 22 – Prompt: Write a poem that spells out the title (acrostic).

Freedom awaits your every decision
Unburden yourself from having an opinion
Calmly take a walk in the opposite direction
Know that no one values your words more than you
Open your mouth just one more time
Find yourself, by yourself, or else
Follow these steps, if you want to live

F. U. C. K. O. F. F.

Question Everything

Quietly, I sit and ponder past mistakes, present circumstances, and
future joys

Quotes from those dead and gone replay in my mind like 80s reruns

Queeny, well she's still here, but not here, her thick Grenadian accent
tells tall tales of my mom growing up

Queasy, I get queasy, when my thoughts lay rest on the "coulda, woulda,
shouldas" of yesterday

Quirky is what they call me for wanting the truth

Quality over quantity is the recipe for success that either gets burned or
just doesn't taste good

Quit waiting for the answers to come find you, because they won't

Question everything and nothing, the answers aren't yours alone.

Day 24 – Prompt: A poem using the words: cake, castle, coral.

Coral Beef

I miss cake
I miss cake, and cookies, and chocolate
Every morning waking up to Bullet Coffee
With no sugar and no creamer
Brown torture in a mug
Starving myself until late afternoon
Drinking more water
My bladder floats on dreams of carbs
I am the queen of my castle
But my fat runs my existence and my home
I just want to eat what I want
I just want to snack when I want
I got beef with this scale
It lurks under my bed
Only to emerge and tell me lies

Day 25 – Prompt: Poem from the perspective of an empty plate.

Coral Beef (Part 2)

Why she ain't eatin'?
All that food her aunts and cousins done cooked
I don't understand
She loves this day almost as much as her birthday
Normally fasting in the morning
Just to fill up in the evening
She'd wear a skirt or stretchy leggings

What the fuck is up?
She's been standing here five minutes holding on to me for dear life
I got beef with these damn diet trends
Just fucking eat already!
She's squeezing me so tight she might force a crack in my coral designs
          (You know her mama bought me on sale 20 years ago)
I know she's hungry, stomach out here talkin' to er'body
She's letting all these damn people, I mean, family, go first

What about me? Fill me up, Bitch!
Oh wait, it's happening, she's reaching
What the fuck?!
It's thanksgiving and all this heifer put on me is salad, turkey, and greens
Nope! I refuse!
See y'all on the other side.
Miss me while I "accidentally" slip from her hands to the waxed tile!

Day 26 – Prompt: Poem about Black Friday.

Shop Till Who Drops

My Black ass will be at home
This Black woman ain't getting pushed, shoved or stepped on
You don't even know how it got its name
My Black money will remain where it is
This Black Friday, feel free to go alone.

Day 27 – Prompt: Haiku about eyes.

Old Ass Eyes

I can't see for shit
Why can't I find my glasses?
They are on my head

Day 28 – Prompt: A poem about poetry.

Ars Poetica

A poem is a poet's lifeline
It's how we speak to the world
Our jumble of metaphors, alliteration, and rhyme
It's our love language, our gift
We offer our everything to you, the reader
Meaning, inspiration, purpose, love
It's all outlined on the page for you
How you interpret it is not our concern
It matters more that you are affected:
       An ounce to do something
       A chasm to speak up
       A whisper to dream in color
A poem is salvation…

              …anchor yourself.

Tomorrow

This is it
The moment I never thought would come
Thirty days of writing
Prompts like literary parents
Checking in every day:
  "Did you write anything?"
  "Have you been keeping up?"
Staying up late to post just before midnight
I can't believe it
This is it
I'm about to write 30 poems in 30 days
Poetry is my name

Day 30 – Prompt: A poem to yourself in gratitude/things you love about yourself.

Glory Be to Me

Blessed is your dark mahogany complexion
Blessed is your ability to speak for the voiceless
Blessed are your black and blue locs
Blessed are your pages which you write upon
Blessed is the love you have for many
Blessed is the fuck you no longer give
Blessed are the lessons you teach
Blessed are the dreams you achieve

NOTES

In November of 2021, I joined a "30 for 30" writing challenge with the marvelous poets and writers of the Write About Now Poetry members groups on Facebook.

It was in celebration of National Novel Writing Month and WAN gave members of the group 10 writing prompts to choose from every day.

This writing challenge turned out to be more than I had hoped it to be. Some days the words were beyond elusive. Other days, the words flowed like rivers.

If you're ever plagued with writer's block, I strongly encourage you to entera writing challenge. You won't be disappointed.

www.ingramcontent.com/pod-product-compliance
Lightning Source LLC
Chambersburg PA
CBHW030528130626
46549CB00007B/3147